KENTUCKY SWAMI

Born on this mountain,
I return many years since.
My Great Plains wife weeps.

KENTUCKY SWAMI

• P O E M S •

Tim Skeen

Winner of the 2001 John Ciardi Prize for Poetry
Selected by Michael Burns

BkMk Press
University of Missouri-Kansas City

BkMk Press
University of Missouri-Kansas City
5101 Rockhill Road
Kansas City, Missouri 64110
(816) 235-2558 (voice)
(816) 235-2611 (fax)
www.umkc.edu/bkmk/
bkmk@umkc.edu

Cover photo, "Flying Ernie," by Tim Skeen

Printed by McNaughton & Gunn, Saline, Michigan.

BkMk Press wishes to thank Michael Burns, Michael Nelson, Philip Miller, Roger Kirschbaum, Karen T. Johnson, Jeannie Irons, Jessica Hylan, & Roxanne M. Witt.

For information about the John Ciardi Prize for Poetry, contact BkMk Press. The prize was first awarded in 1999 to Steve Gehrke for *The Resurrection Machine,* selected by Miller Williams.

Library of Congress Cataloging-in-Publication Data

Skeen, Tim, 1959-
    Kentucky Swami / Tim Skeen.
        p. cm.
    ISBN 1-886157-33-2
      1. Kentucky—Poetry. I. Title.

PS3619,K44 K4 2001
811'.6—dc21
                     2001037546

10   9   8   7   6   5   4   3   2   1

CONTENTS

I

A History 11
Graphite 12
Strike 13
The Cabin 15
How I Got My Name 16
The Voice of a Woman with One Lung 17
Elton Maynard 18
Kentucky Swami 19
Painting the Dresser 20
Fragment for an Elegy 21
The Instructor at the Police Academy Teaches
      the Come-Along 22
Signing Up for Unemployment Benefits 23
Scar 24
Systemic Lupus 25
9800 Franklin Avenue 26

II

Tongue 31
Biljana 32
Rural 34
Tomatoes 35
Gameday Saturday Afternoon 36
Jehovah's Witnesses 38
1 Place Denfert-Rochereau 39
Patrick Lowell Putnam's Monologue 41
Tai Chi Chuan 44
The American Red Cross 45
Buck Owens and His Buckaroos in Japan! 49
For My Wife on Our Six-Week Anniversary 50
The Sunken Garden 52
The King of Garlic 53

III

Directions to the Otter Creek Correctional Facility   57

A Commonwealth of Kentucky #2 Pencil   58

War Memorial in Wheelwright, Kentucky   59

To Another Student Who Forgot to Put a Name on
       His Paper   60

At the Gulf War Veteran's Funeral   61

The Lancaster Room   62

She Asks If I Love Her   63

The Unmet Needs   64

Public Works   65

Found Poem from a Book in a Box of Books I Sold to a
       Novel Idea Before Moving to Kentucky Again   66

Safe-T-Man   67

The Masonry Professor at the Community College   68

To Our Unborn Child   70

To the Driver Who Took My Reserved Parking Space #53   71

Translation of a Mathematical Equation Which I Found on
       a Blackboard   72

The Last Century Seen as a Used Book   74

For the Record   75

for Ray Ronci

ACKNOWLEDGMENTS

The Antioch Review: Scar.

The Book of Kentucky, Kent Fielding and Dave Poorman, eds.: The Voice of a Woman with One Lung.

Coffee & Chicory: Born on This Mountain (epigraph to book).

Coffeehouse Poets' Quarterly: Tomatoes.

Columbia: A Magazine of Poetry and Prose: The Cabin.

Confluence: 9800 Franklin Avenue.

The Cut-Thru Review: Translation of a Mathematical Equation Which I Found on a Blackboard; Signing Up for Unemployment Benefits.

The Journal of Kentucky Studies: Biljana.

Kudzu: Buck Owens and His Buckaroos in Japan; The Unmet Needs.

Laurus: To Another Student Who Forgot to Put a Name on His Paper.

Mediphors: Systemic Lupus.

Mid-American Review: Gameday Saturday Afternoon.

Milkweed Review: Patrick Lowell Putnam's Monologue; Public Works.

New Voices: University and College Poetry Prizes (Academy of American Poets), Donald Hall, ed.: A History; How I Got My Name.

opticmagazine.com: The American Red Cross; Rural; Safe-T-Man.

Pikeville Review: To My Wife on Our Six-Week Anniversary; To the Driver Who Took My Reserved Parking Space #53.

Prairie Schooner: 1 Place Denfert-Rochereau; At the Gulf War Veteran's Funeral; The King of Garlic; To Our Unborn Child; War Memorial in Wheelwright, Kentucky.

Sonora Review: She Asks If I Love Her.

Sugar Mule: The Masonry Professor at the Community College.

Time All Over, Adrian Swain, ed.: The Last Century Seen as a Used Book.

I would like to thank Susan Atefat-Peckham, Julianna Baggott, Steve Blume, Judy Bowen, Michael Collier, Howard Ellis, The Kentucky Arts Council, Robert Kibler, Philip Levine, Comrade Biljana Obradovic, Joel Peckham, Stanley Plumly, Kim Ports, Prestonsburg Community College, Mike Puican, Hilda Raz, James Reiss, Pattianne Rogers, Ray Ronci, Joshu Sasaki Roshi, Billy Skeen, Iris Skeen, Nola Mae Skeen, Marcia Southwick, Pamela Stewart, David St. John, Judy Weiner, Ken Weiner, and my wife, Pam Weiner.

I

A HISTORY

My father takes me to the basement
and shows me the jar of corn that was canned
during the Depression when he was five.
He tells me the day was hot in Floyd County,

and locusts sang from the pine-covered hills
while he carried wood for the stove and water
to boil the jars. The pile of shucks rose
on the porch, and Roosevelt spoke on the radio.

His mother, he says, was beautiful.
I nod my head yes.
I have seen the pictures.
I do not tell my father how the summer before

she died, Granny showed me the jar of corn,
showed me the scar across her palm she got
when the knife slipped. She had sent him to find
Pa-dad who drank the money from his alphabet job

and passed out in the coalhouse. She said
my father hugged her close, told her he loved her.
Then always this jar of corn,
too bitter to eat, too valuable to throw away.

GRAPHITE

I'm mowing the yard
when the wind suddenly shifts
from the direction of U.S. Steel.
The sun catches the graphite flecks
and makes the world sparkle like it does
sometimes when you stand up too fast.
The place where my father works
darkens our lungs. The trees, the car,
the house, the street, the mower,
the hair on my body all shine
the same dull light. I brush up
against the door and leave behind a smear
like a line erased by the fat pencils
with which we learned to write.

STRIKE

to Billy

You're right, the mill never missed
your paycheck. Thirty years
and never a mistake.
You're a simple man, as you say.

It's beyond us if ore's piled on the docks
as high as a couple
of telephone poles end on end,
if the Japanese produce

more and better,
if the vascular-like bed of oil pipe
around the world is contracting,
it's beyond us if the war in Vietnam gave you years

of overtime and taught you
that the price of everything is time
spent rolling the seamless pipe
from the furnaces to flatbed trucks.

My bicycle, for instance, cost you ten hours.
Sure, you work hard, take credit
for good work, responsibility for bad.
Listen, think of Sisyphus—

no, no, mythology is no help in this.
Or maybe the history of labor,
of Cesar Chavez and the farmworkers,
others who wear union caps like you,

how a small group of itinerant workers
fought to overcome . . .
All right. Just promise me this:
when the police tap you on the shoulder

and say come along, unlock
your arms from the arms next to you and go.
Your name on the police blotter is their crime.
Have nothing in your pockets

except a union card.
Answer all they ask of you
in simple, raw-material language,
coal to coke to ore to steel.

Don't struggle against the handcuffs.
No one knows better than you
what they are made of.
Know that I am your son who loves you,

and I'll be waiting at the station
to pick you up,
to read the police report to you.
Let that be my work.

THE CABIN

My father went away for two weeks the winter
after burying a son to build on this hundred acres
of pinewood. He drew the plans on the back

of a Beechnut bag, laying it out so he could work
alone. He carried the studs, plywood sheets, nails,
and blocks in the back of his pickup. I sit

on a stump and drag my feet in pine chips,
imagining how he learned to appreciate the pines
because they are the green of the woods

and easily loaned their resinous souls to his ax.
The cabin tilts a little to one side.
In his grief he drove the nails too deeply

into the wood. Yet only the glass
in the windows seems less permanent than
the nettle-covered earth. Even the hunters,

who tear down fences and dump plastic bags
filled with beer cans along the roads, must have been
grateful for a place to hold off the cold.

Before leaving, they swept the floor
and left the broom standing in a corner.

HOW I GOT MY NAME

I think my great-grandfather's name
was Castle, though nobody's sure.
He got off a coal train long enough
to leave an illiterate woman with a child,
Juanita, touched with bad luck.
Once her Model T lost its brakes
coming off Clinch Mountain. She made it

all the way to the bottom,
only to hit a miner's wife in town.
I remember she took me to watch
one of the last steam trains.
Where did they all go? I asked.
Away, she answered. I watched the engineer's
tired face lean out of the engine,

his back against a known point of origin,
coal from Kentucky, cars from Detroit,
change in his oily pocket.
One autumn day in 1958, laid off with a bad back,
Juanita brought a handful of grass to my mother
and told her, if it's a boy, name him Timothy,
after something common, something always near.

THE VOICE OF A WOMAN
WITH ONE LUNG

It speaks of Bakelite,
high humidity,
and carbide lamps,
of the washing machine
on the porch, gravel roads and dust.
It speaks of her 1959

Dodge Seneca Chief, a 454
cubic inch whine, push button
dashboard and tail fins.
Knocked out of gear once,
the car rolls.
I hang onto the door,

my father runs alongside,
gets a foot on the brake,
her scream like a police whistle.
It speaks of Pall Malls,
of black coffee each morning
cooled, then slurped from a saucer,

of digitalis swallowed
with an exaggerated gulp.
It speaks of the AARP,
a husband hard of hearing
from the World War,
of a house too small.

It speaks of veterans' benefits
and social security.
When she dies, they bury her
with a light blue scarf the color
of smoke around the hole
in her throat.

ELTON MAYNARD

I never find the baseball.
Elton dies of the bourbon,
years after my grandfather,
in a home in Lexington, Kentucky.
I don't find my way to the funeral.

Sometimes when Elton drinks
he stops by my grandfather's house
and wants to throw the baseball with me.
He takes my brother's glove,
too small for his hand,

makes his way carefully among the crawdad holes,
and pitches,
at first careful and slow,
then faster and wilder
with each exaggerated windup.

He leans his head far back to suck the air
like a shot of liquor.
I concentrate on the sweat
under his armpits,
the red letters on his blue shirt, ELTON,

and step further away each time he throws,
until my hand stings,
until he's as far away as I can throw,
until my grandfather stands up from his lawnchair
and I let the ball go by me

into the weeds.
Cursing me for stepping aside,
Elton looms heavy nearby
while I stomp through the high grass
with my blind feet.

KENTUCKY SWAMI

My father cuts his fingers pulling off
rusty tin underpinning from the shed.
He hasn't stopped to put on the gloves.
A strike with the claw hammer, a pull
with the bare hand, then a sizing up
of a new sheet of galvanized tin.

It's always the same lesson, his Appalachian
childhood and mine: if we can't make it,
we have to do without; if we can make it,
then we have to accept corners slightly
out of square and lines almost level.
His fingers leave streaks on bright metal.

PAINTING THE DRESSER

I'd been hired to move dirt
from the front yard to the back,

but the owner's wife needs someone
who could re-do furniture.

I am someone. She looks after the nanny
who looks after the children. I feel sorry

for her. She studies in a cabin
to pass the Ohio bar exam. She has

a place waiting at her husband's law firm.
I spend two days on my knees.

I hold the can of varnish as far away
from my face as I can. I try

not to spill anything on the drop cloth.
Finally, it's the strokes of my brush that

get me fired. She wants them to run
up and down. Vertical brush strokes,

of course. I'm stupid. She refuses
to pay my boss for my labor.

He'd have to spend more to collect
than he'd make from the job.

It's not worth it. The logic's plain.
The lines run down. Down. And down.

FRAGMENT FOR AN ELEGY
for Ernie, 1960-1982

He makes his living
with the muscles in his arms
and cuts his beard trim

as a two-by-four.
One summer,
I help him pull

down a house,
plank by plank, brick by brick.
We start on the roof

in June,
slowly undressing the empty
spaces inside,

until in August,
I watch him on his knees,
sifting the cool earth

under the foundation
through his fingers
that find an old license plate,

animal bones,
and a few broken bottles
to hold him over

until the next job.

THE INSTRUCTOR AT THE POLICE ACADEMY
TEACHES THE COME-ALONG

Approach the subject from behind.
Grasp your nightstick in the middle,
very hard, in your weak hand—
this is very important.
Make sure the leather thong's
loose around the thumb
so that in the event
the subject turns around
and takes the stick away,
you can reach for your pistol.
Keeping the nightstick parallel
with your forearm, thrust it
between the subject's legs,
then turn your wrist
so that the stick
and your arm form a "T"
in front of his genitals.
With your other hand grab his shoulder
and lift as hard as you can
with both arms.
Now the subject will go
where you want him to.
Remember, he is not your brother!
He's scum, a dirtbag,
a frog, asshole, perp,
fuck up, slimeball,
squirrel, a 10-08.
Don't be timid!

SIGNING UP FOR UNEMPLOYMENT BENEFITS

At the Lorain Bureau of Employment,
I show the clerks my army discharge papers
and fill out the forms they give me
which explain how I've been defending

the right to earn the minimum wage.
I move from one line to another
and wait to show my paperwork to people
with jobs who tell me about the opportunities

in Corrections for ex-MPs.
I fill out more color-coded forms
under the fluorescent lights.
Before I joined the army, this building

used to be a grocery store.
I examine each form as carefully as day-old bread,
sign my name exactly the same way each time.
Somebody behind me shakes

hands with a buddy in another line.
Ronald Reagan wears a hard hat and a flannel shirt
on TV. He promises to put us all to work.
Faithfully, I carry my blue record book

each week from one factory to another,
collecting signatures, stamps, and numbers
that explain everything
except why I do not have a job.

SCAR

Barbara's was like a tattoo
with a motive, a thin translucent line
connecting her navel
to the darker pubic hair. In bed
sometimes, both of us a little drunk,
she'd take my index finger
and rub the scar, holding it
not like the child's game, to make
the hurt go away, but as if my fingernail
were the blade of a scalpel.
She never spoke then,
but looking away, was alone.
Maybe she was thinking
of her daughter asleep at her sister's.
Maybe she was thinking of her ex-husband,
the friend from school, the cop
who specialized in sex crimes
and screwed everyone
he could. I looked at her long hair,
the gentle muscles of her arms,
her breasts, the smooth blonde
of her body. I had just got out
of the army. I was twenty-one.
The scar marked the marred world
of our stillness. I touched it,
precise and dependable as nothing else
in our lives.

SYSTEMIC LUPUS

The rash is only the body's way
of holding onto fire. Everybody agrees
Nola's done exactly that for years.
She washes the windows at the end
of March and I say,
"You'd better get down off that stool.
You'll catch a cold."
None of us know she's already sick.
She sweats, then chills over the stove,
over the ironing,
but she shakes her head, smiles, and keeps on.
When she goes out, she carries her own
drinking water to go with the pills.
She's outlived her parents,
four brothers, a son, and stray dogs
named for their mongrel passing:
Tinker, Tamper, Shaggy.
Why can't she accept this gradual slowing down?
Why can't she outlast this burning across
her face, this disease so frightened of her
even the medical books admit it comes
disguised as a butterfly?

9800 FRANKLIN AVENUE

Just when we could find
our way through the woods
behind the tool shed,
round and turreted like a tower,

just when we could find
the blossoming dogwood and listen
to our own voices rising
again into Sunday school sincerity,

and just when we could name
the neighbor's dogs, Sidney
and Bunky, Tiny and Spice,
then we found the white wing

opened on a rock
like a handkerchief left
to dry in the sun. Too clean
for the work of the dogs, you said,

and buried it there.
But soon after, it seemed
as if the legs of chairs snapped
at my toes in the dark,

the spot of oil on the driveway
became a slick,
and I began to lock
the bedroom door at night.

Not one of our neighbors,
neither Barbara nor Chuck,
could tell me why
that happiness ended.

Nor could our parents,
though they remembered where
and when theirs did. Living alone
in a prairie city a thousand miles away,

I remember the wing,
so heavy with grief it pulled
down that beautiful house held between
the ivy's knocked knees.

II

TONGUE

Before antilock brakes and air bags, when Patrick Bedard
was writing in *Car & Driver* about the inanity of seatbelt laws,

my thin face met the windshield of a Chrysler K-Car.
The end of my tongue and a tooth rode to the hospital

in a paramedic's breast pocket. They could not be saved.
With my jaw in an Erich Arch Bar Wire Brace, I learned again to listen,

really listen, to the rounded sounds of vowels and the angular consonants:
bowel, think, piece, write, me, wind, slum, classic, boy, girl.

Sometimes, with no one else around, I still hear phantom words
called out to me at odd moments like the fifth voice in a quartet.

The hungry twang of the Appalachian drawl, the bald-tire diphthongs of
          the plains,
I know they're from my own unaccounted for piece of tongue yearning

to be reunited with the mouth into which it was born.
I listen, mimic its every word, and listening, learn to speak again.

BILJANA

The country where you were born
ceased to exist
the day you arrived in America,
and your passport
with its six sheaths of wheat,
one for each of the warring republics,
won't let you back home,
and won't let you stay here.
Think of the walks we've had,
and the flowers,
how, each spring, you can't resist
taking a sprig
of lily of the valley.
No one will miss one tiny flower,
you say. I'm going
to miss the oak tree outside your window,
the stains on your carpet,
the salty meat dishes,
even your neighbor's barking dog
when you leave this place
for your next temporary home.
I know
what it's like to have no place to go.
There's a five-story bank
with an elevator where
my family's home used to be
in Pikeville, Kentucky.
Where I scraped Tonka roads out of the side of the mountain
with my brother,
there's the new Route 23. He's been dead
for many years now.
Up north, few understood his Appalachian accent.
You never tire
of hearing about him, and I never tire

of listening
about your grandfather's plum trees
and the way he makes *slivovitz,*
homemade brandy, or your niece
and nephew, whose names
I've only just now learned how to pronounce: *Dusan* and *Dusica.*
The word Balkanite means hillbilly.

RURAL

On my knees, I brush the gnats
away from her ass. She turns
her face back toward me. Her breasts
brush the black soil. Who'd believe
I don't want to be here? "Relax,"
she grimaces with pleasure, "no one's
gonna see us." I know she's right.
I smell summer between her legs. Heat rises
from the plowed earth. The southern Ohio
evening lasts only a moment. In the distance,
at the edge of the soybean field, a barn
falls in on its own shadow.

TOMATOES

The woman I used to live with grows tomatoes.
Their roots nearly broke the clay pots
on her windowsills before she got them
into the ground. Now they're full of August heat,

swelled with humidity, ripe with the aquifer.
She can't be blamed for planting late—
it's my fault, I admit it, I regret it.
So I'm grateful when she gives me sacks

of tomatoes. But I can't eat them all.
Tomatoes fill my refrigerator. I eat them
with bread and mayonnaise, with fish, with tuna,
with sauces and pasta,

with beans and rice, rice and beans.
I think seriously about freezing tomatoes.
I am sick of tomatoes, of summer, of humidity.
My punishment takes the form of tomatoes.

Can I be blamed if I wouldn't touch them
as a child, if my mother still has rows
of canned tomatoes in her basement?
I eat what I can, and the rest I take to Ray,

my friend who's divorced this summer.
Take these, my friend, I say to him.
He does, but tells me his refrigerator
is full, too, gifts from his ex-wife.

In January I may miss tomatoes,
but now I have
a refrigerator full,
Ray at his house, me at mine.

GAMEDAY SATURDAY AFTERNOON

I smile at the man dropping a letter
into the mailbox, the young girls
leaving the William Penn Apartments,
even the kid in the parking garage booth,
though he's watching the game on TV.
These afternoons cut out and sweep
more leisurely than all others.
So much enthusiasm in the stadium
seems to bodyblock the rest of the city.
Just to walk, to look up
at the Cessna, dragging GO BIG RED:
GO BIG RED on the bumpers of Caprice, Ninety-eight, and Coup de Ville,
GO BIG RED at the College of Hair Design,
GO BIG RED in the window of the Sweep Left Restaurant, Lounge and
        Sports Club,
GO BIG RED at the Night Before,
GO BIG RED at the Foxy Lady,
GO BIG RED Barrymore's,
GO BIG RED O'Rourke's,
GO BIG RED at the Steak House and Stoney Inn,
GO BIG RED on the door of the Trophy Shop,
GO BIG RED chant the cheerleaders on TV,
GO BIG RED at Ralph's Hungry Eye Tattoo Studio & Gun Sales,
GO BIG RED Greek Shop,
GO BIG RED Cookbook,
GO BIG RED Keno,
GO BIG RED at Harold Otey's execution,
GO BIG RED shouts GO BUSH/QUAYLE,
VIVA EL ROJO GRANDE,
GO BIG RED August,
GO BIG RED September,
GO BIG RED October,
GO BIG RED November,
GO BIG RED December,

oh yes,
especially December,
GO BIG RED over the nativity scenes,
surrounded with red flags bearing "N"
which stands for Nebraska.

JEHOVAH'S WITNESSES

The black woman's tinted designer glasses
are too large, like the porch on my small house.
The white woman smiles, her purse held like a baby
on her hip. They tell me they're here

on important work—do I have a little spare time?—
the last words spoken the way the words spare change
are spoken by people who demand it.
Across the street a man waits behind the wheel

of a white Chevy Suburban. Jehovah's servants
are very practical. In the yard the white flowers
of the crab apple and the blooms of the redbud tree
compete like opposing evangelical ministers.

Why am I so speechless right now,
the one week out of the year when these trees flower?
If I could explain to these ladies, if only words
and good intentions could come to me as effortlessly

as these blossoms to spring!
Here comes *The Watchtower* from the purse.
Their words seem to be coming from a high,
crenelated redoubt. I, too, have important work:

The used book from A Novel Idea,
Desert Boneyard, which I need to read quickly
so I can get it in the mail in time for Father's Day,
and my turkey soup, which evolved each day this week

from roast turkey to drumsticks, to turkey salad, to soup,
sit on the table next to a slice of bread.

1 PLACE DENFERT-ROCHEREAU

Parfait Amour is made of the bitter zest of limes,
spirit of roses and spicy odors.
You pick up a bottle and put it in your pocket.
Walking all day, we'd seen everything from our feet,
covering the catacombs as if we had bloodhounds behind us.
So many have been dug up to make room for others
above ground, and I suppose just to make room.

The bones are stacked behind mortared walls of skulls
and legs, behind stones with poetry and axioms.
One says, "Behold the common end of great projects."
Miles of this. Entire cemeteries dug up during
the eighteenth and nineteenth centuries, all the flesh
remaining in the topsoil. Water seeps through the limestone

shafts, through the graveled path, then to where?
A sculpture of a cathedral carved in the rock,
a well with a staircase winding into perfectly still,
green water, into infinity. How can you want children
in spite of the ossuaries of this world? Could you
bring the meat of humanity into this world?
Will we ever marry? These bones were once children.

To know we're brought into the world under terms beyond
our own volition, and yet to be so hopeful. Amour?
You didn't see the tears come to my eyes, the tears
in van Gogh's room at the *Musée d'Orsay*, the same tears
which welled up on the *Boulevard Sebestopol* when, as I walked by,
a worker with a high pressure hose forced wads of toilet paper

from a two franc public toilet down the evacuation hole,
while a woman about our age called to me from a half-open
doorway for a cigarette. *Je suis de passage.* And you

and everyone. The resistance stored art objects here
during the war to keep them out of German hands.
People have wandered down and become lost, perhaps
looking on a van Gogh or Renoir, never to be seen again.

Miles and miles. Kilometers and kilometers.
The conscience of Paris, rusting iron gates closed off
from the twenty-six franc tour. *Cimetière L'Enfants.*
The *hors de combat* of the revolution. The tubercular hospital.
The designer of the catacombs, the designer of Paris.
Everyone's here. The bones of people are resilient objects,

so unlike the bones of one-legged pigeons. The knuckles
of the femur stack well one atop another, and it's a long bone.
A surprisingly long bone. So much rocklike stuff underneath
all that flesh. All that sweet, beautiful living—
I wish my brother were buried closer, but then why?
This caffeine headache, this tiny tibula lodged oddly
out of place in the middle of my brain. Why did the *clochard*

under the *Pont Neuf* stand at attention and give an exaggerated salute?
Ici tomba un soldat pour le libération de Paris.
To come above ground, exhausted, off balance, thirsty, lost
in another part of the city, is to mistake these bones
for *Parfait Amour*, made of the bitter zest of limes,
spirit of roses and spicy odors.

PATRICK LOWELL PUTNAM'S MONOLOGUE*

The fetus's leg extends from Abanzima's
birth canal and seems to kick the inside
of her thigh. She says it's been dead three days.
The medicine man refuses to help
and will not leave until he's given more
elephant meat. He's an ironic character,
like this baby, a pygmy too big to be born.
How can I turn Abanzima away?
Her mother and her father sing songs
as they wait outside:
The sky is far, a place where
no grass grows on which to lie.
Yet children are conceived in heaven;
they will feed us in old age.
How purposeless the world is. Dr. Stedman
at Harvard used to say that, and he flunked me
in composition. Pointless. If she dies . . .
I'm not a doctor. I'm an *Agent Sanitaire*,
and how I had to plead with the Belgian Red Cross
for the title. It took my father's doing
and the long reach of the Lowell name to win
the privilege of dressing wounds and setting bones,
delivering babies dead and alive in Africa.
Poor father. He's never understood.
But what should I expect from a man who
can't tell the difference between the sweet flavor
of the African ant and the sour, hazy taste
of the American? The few weeks he was here
he boiled every drop of water, took his quinine
by the watch, and never left his pith helmet
out of sight. Still, I love that man.
All the mistakes I've made, and in his eyes
am making, and yet we know how much
our relationship means. I don't care about
war bonds and rubber trees. My God, how I try

to forget Boston. Each night I listen
to the monkeys in the trees and I think
to myself, Boston, how grateful I am
that you're not here. Father, don't you understand?
If you were here now, you'd do the same.
Of course he couldn't stay, I didn't want him
to really. What would he do with Abanzima?
He's too much the Christian to turn her away.
Me? I could just as easily look the other way
and get the medicine man to share a drink.
He loves gin and cigarettes. Oh . . . I'll help,
because it pleases me to do so, the way
it pleased me to swim the Longgele River,
aptly named, by God, and build my hut
in this clearing white and hot under the sun.
Six years I've been here. Six years, and home
to Boston only once, when mother was ill.
Sure, I've had visitors. That woman from
the *New Yorker*, who stayed a couple of days
and got everything wrong in her article.
She wasn't shocked that I'd taken a native wife.
I'll give her that. But that I had three wives,
she couldn't accept. Damned if I'll write
one word to explain myself to anybody!
Old Percival Lowle, arriving in America
from Bristol at the age of 68, bringing
two sons and a daughter, with their families,
he'd understand. America must have looked
like Africa then. Poor Percival, until
the Revolution brought profit in the holds
of the British merchant ships that fell to his fleet
of commerce raiders. By and by the Lowells
got too rich to need slaves and they freed them all.
Great-uncle James Russell Lowell, cousin Amy.
But I don't want to talk about them. I am here.

Prince Leopold and Princess Astrid of Belgium
came here to see me. What a night we had,
dancing with the pygmies, eating wild mushrooms,
honey, smoking marijuana, yodeling!
Oh . . . I am tired. First morphine for Abanzima,
now morphine for me. Connect the headlight
to the car battery and light the paraffin lamps.
The lemurs in their cages, the horned viper
and the cobra watch. My tools scissors, pliers,
wire cutters, sleep. Sleep Abanzima.
Slowly pull the fetus's leg straight out
and snip. Through the soft bone, close to the groin.
Reach in, push up. Now an arm. Reach in, turn,
pull the other leg and cut. The opposite
of God, I turn the child into nothing.
Pull. The head is large. Come to the world.
The wire cutters. O God, here is your baby,
nameless, headless, legless, armless, streamlined
so that the pain of this world has nothing to latch onto,
resembling its own shriveled afterbirth, a boy.

*Inspired by Joan Mark's book *The King of the World in
the Land of the Pygmies*

TAI CHI CHUAN
for Helen Tao

She stretches her arms in front
of her face and says, breathe.

I stretch my arms in front of my face, and breathe.
When she bends her knees, I bend my knees.

At first we move together: ward off
to the left, ward off to the right,

brush the knee. But the wild horse's mane
I comb with my hands is not her horse.

The monkey I repulse is more determined
to kill me than her monkey.

Now the golden cock stands on one leg,
and she is in a world where

the needle at the bottom of the sea
is not lost forever,

where the window opens to a mountain,
and the woman who works the shuttle is fair.

I am ill at ease in this large room.
The ceiling fans are as out of rhythm

as I am. No golden cock.
I'm tired of talking.

I try to show her I love her,
bending my knees, stretching my arms:

chimney smoke under pine trees,
the cat flicks its tail.

THE AMERICAN RED CROSS

1. The Flooded Town

Thunderstorms give some kind of warning,
some shaking or cast of light,
an itch like the survivors

of the Johnstown Flood felt
before the dam gave way.
There seems no point opening

the umbrella what with mud climbing
the steps of every building in town.
The National Guard MPs look too rested

to be from here. They tell me
not to drive the Red Cross truck
over standing water. It could be sewage.

Thunder echoes down Water Street.
The people whose town this is
have already laid aside pens and pencils,

knives and forks, their faces raised
up through windows and doorways.
This is the stagnant moment that accompanies

the stalled front. How many fire ants
in the writhing scum that floats
toward the open door? The tractors

are parked in the barns, the football camp
has closed early, planes hold
to the ground. These late storm clouds,

only one percent water, will move north.
Under the mud, the manhole covers
are worn as smooth as silver quarters

by the thumbing of tires. All over town
construction pits are filled with water.
In the distance a siren wails.

The town wails back.

2.   Bleach

stacks floor to ceiling,
6 one-gallon jugs

to a cardboard case,
now and then turned soggy

by a loose lid.
Shipped on pallets, wrapped

in plastic, piled
This End Up, it cleans

the mud one cup to the bucket,
purifies the wells

one jug apiece.
Each time the Mississippi floods

bleach appears
along with head colds, short hair,

catfish fattened in the pools
of cornfields.

Bleach kills the mosquitoes' droning,
and when the schools reopen,

along with the snare drums
of the marching bands,

there will be the smell
of bleach.

3.   Song and Recitation

The bell is lyrical,
repetition plays a part.
A tornado visits Thayer County,
Nebraska, once every 3.2 years.
The bell is lyrical.
Luckily, no one dies,

so I can tell everything.
The poor mobile home
split, then slammed
into the creek bed
only adds to the confusion.
I turn away and walk

into the muddy cornfield
toward the rusty pump.
I'm not from around here.
Perhaps that's how I know
its water is miraculous.
One drink and this life,

this death, are no different.
I smell the raw sewage
from the ruptured pipe,

and face the cow that hangs
in a row of windbreak trees.
To the left there's Rural Route 3,

dressed in scattered clothes.
To the right the demolished Gilead Church.
I didn't walk into this mud hole
looking for a miracle,
say last year's dried yellow jackets
in the storm windows come back

to life in this amazing wind.
I simply came looking for the church bell.
I recite, "Here's the dell!
Where the hell is the bell?"
The cow in the tree moves.
Its bell is lyrical.

BUCK OWENS AND HIS BUCKAROOS IN JAPAN!
found poem

This monophonic,
microgroove
33 1/3 rpm recording
is playable
on monophonic
and stereo phonographs
that provide outstanding
sound reproduction.

It will continue
to be a source
of the finest
monophonic performance.
When played on any phonograph,
it cannot become obsolete.

FOR MY WIFE ON OUR SIX-WEEK ANNIVERSARY

Mac's shattered teeth can be pulled,
and the wire holding his jaw in unnatural stillness
will be removed. Let's say the injuries
are consistent with the ice-covered streets
and the dusk color of his fur, the late hours
and a difficult drive from one minimum wage job

to another, from daycare to the IGA in a car
without a muffler. It could have been worse,
after all. A man I once called friend described
how he swerved, not to avoid but to hit a cat
along a rural Ohio roadside, and hit it he did,
the intestines flying loose.

Our small house still protects us on the solid corner
of Washington and 14th Streets. The porch
can be screened and Mac will sit again in the breezy
sunlight. We have one of the best vets. Medicine
dropper, drop by drop, we'll have to feed him,
but wrapped in a towel under my arm, day by day,

he'll grow stronger. So, too, you and I. It's not
the same world for a cat as it is for a child.
It is. But it isn't. And what if it is?
Years ago my jaw smashed against a windshield
with the force of the breakers off Coronado Island,
where we spent our honeymoon. Like the waves,

I retreated, reformed, retreated again, reformed,
and learned to speak in a more compassionate voice.
And you have suffered in your secret way.
I knew we'd marry when you showed me the yearbooks
with your photos blotted out by your own hand.
Our first act beyond what each alone is capable of

is to save the life of your chucklehead cat,
warming the medicine dropper of tuna broth between
our thighs, husband and wife, three good eyes
and sixty-three teeth between us.

THE SUNKEN GARDEN

On adjacent poles one flag blows north, the other south.
Two sparrows try to make a nest out of an open mailbox.
I worry that this sudden, late March freeze

will kill the first crocuses, only faint colors
against the Alberta Clipper, yellows, whites,
after so long the Great Plains winter.

The shadows of branches make an incomprehensible graffiti.
Hold on, I remind myself, the sunshine will come like handfuls
of cinnamon bread thrown under the trees.
The ears of a cat, serrated by a dozen cat fights,

look like the greening tips of brown leaves.
Underground, the eggs of insects swell.
A millennium of arrowheads rise
toward the marble water girl.

THE KING OF GARLIC

to Tim and Vero

I wave your garlic plant
like a skinny scepter
from one side of this life
to the other,

blessing everyone
flying overhead from place to place.
Skeptical? So am I.
But you are in bed

after your wedding feast
while I walk through the garden.
The blinking lights from the plane
trace my path from the plains

to the mountains,
a leftover fish wrapped in foil
under my other arm.

III

DIRECTIONS TO THE OTTER CREEK CORRECTIONAL FACILITY

When the guards clear my classroom for an evening recount,
I step outside and stand near the fence.

Here are years of cigarette butts casually flicked
into the rolls of concertina wire. No one can reach

in there to clean them up. I take strength from the cigarette butts.
In Kentucky, tobacco plants receive a lot of tough love

by having their blossoms pinched off to strengthen the leaves.
Beyond the fence, the wall of the mountain rises straight up

like a lump on the head a police baton might leave.
Here are the loneliest men in America. Some things help, I guess.

The bags of magazines, the books I bring in.
Each week before I'm allowed through the gate, I answer the same question:

Do you have any weapons, drugs, or contraband on your person?
I admit it was uncomfortable at first, but it's routine now

like washing your hands after using the toilet.
How have so many in America found their way here?

Through the whorehouses of Okinawa, which are a kind of prison.
Through having been shot at four times, and four times missed.

Through the broken window of a liquor store.
Through the sincere love of alcohol, marijuana and other drugs.

Through junk cars, bad luck, and poverty, poverty, poverty.
Blue jays fly in and out of the yard with impunity. This must hurt to watch.

A COMMONWEALTH OF KENTUCKY #2 PENCIL

A deep blue affair with white lettering, the kind of lettering
popular on 1920s typewriters. And the eraser's white rubber
better resists the sun's brittling than the common stuff, an eraser

worthy of Pound's dictum to the historians: keep your erasers
in order. This pencil holds a point better than any other,
and when it needs sharpening the slim body perfectly fits

into the hole of the sharpener. Turning the handle,
I imagine I'm operating a lathe, honing the brilliant ash
of a Louisville Slugger, a home run in every flick of the wrist.

For writing fiction, this pencil has no equal. The words
and the metaphors flow like well water from the hand pump.
But when I try to write facts, that in Floyd County

40% of the residents over the age of 25 have not finished
high school, I feel the pencil point dull. The words
on the page, which began so clear and precise,

become smudged and illegible.
I rub my eyes, sharpen and resharpen the pencil,
but the point melts away into shavings,

and I become like the grandfathers of Floyd County,
whittling away at oak sticks on front porches,
chewing Beechnut tobacco, saying nothing at all.

WAR MEMORIAL IN WHEELWRIGHT, KENTUCKY

Up the hollow, past the Otter Creek prison, the U.S. flag
claims each name screwed to the plaque

like a monogram on a handkerchief.
This poor mining town has earned the right to brag,

and honor, unlike company scrip, cannot be taken back.
Is there a lonelier place in America? I am silent with grief

at the thought of these ghosts who once lingered at the mouths
of a dozen numbered mines to smoke a last cigarette

and bow their heads before stepping into oblivion.
Explosions, natural gas, roof falls, black lung, familiar deaths

of all sorts awaited them underground, so they gladly risked a bet
and left for wars imagined and uncertain:

Chester Johnson, Charles Hall, Curtis Sizemore, Floyd Blackburn,
Dewey Lester, Tilton Little, Howard Price, Clay Taulbee, Gomer
        Blackburn.

TO ANOTHER STUDENT WHO FORGOT
TO PUT A NAME ON HIS PAPER

You thank me for assigning this paper
because you "appreciate the opportunity
to communicate real emotions in writting."
You worked hard all summer on a farm,
didn't get along with your father. Also,
you write that your writing needs improvement,
and you hope I can help.
It's as if you've become my brother, Ernie,
the kid in the back when the teachers give up,
the kid who says nothing in class,
who sees out of the window fields of marijuana,
money to be made. Whoever you are,
next time please write your name on your paper
so I will recognize you.

AT THE GULF WAR VETERAN'S FUNERAL
for Fran and Kaitlyn

He told me he didn't realize he'd been wounded.
After they'd run through the sand from one position
to another, his buddy pointed to the blood oozing
from the tattered leg of his camouflaged utilities
and yelled for a corpsman. Morphine followed,
then the quiet ride to the hospital ship where the doctor

removed the shrapnel. You're going to be OK,
someone told him. The Purple Heart was harder than a scab,
and something to be proud of. For the next eight years,
he was one of the strongest men in the gym. I would watch,
astonished, as he curled the impossible dumbbells one
after the other, maintaining a casual cadence while he swapped

one for one his wartime marine stories for my peacetime army stories.
Seven hundred thousand pounds of depleted uranium shells
were fired in the Gulf. Each shell burned like a tiny Chernobyl.
Destroyed vehicles had to be buried in place.
The sicker he became the less he stuttered. When he laughed,
I thought of two bullets rattling around the bottom of a can.

Even if we didn't know it, now I understand what he was telling me.
This foreign cancer was the real enemy. Set after set, repetition
after repetition, he fortified himself against the threat
that had been made in the desert: If I have to crawl thousands
of miles on my hands and knees, over the oceans, across the plains,
even to the faraway country of eastern Kentucky, I will come.

THE LANCASTER ROOM

The man holds his head in his hands
when no one's looking, elbows on the table.
He moves deliberately, each word and gesture
as if read from a prompter. His son moves in
with the video camera, and the man smiles
not at all shyly, says again how well he feels,
and isn't it great to have so many family
and friends at table on this sixtieth birthday.
This man with a new liver, who used
to be behind the camera, who insisted on close-ups
of all the children around motel pools,
tells his son be sure to get it all,
come in real close, be sure to get the cards.
He holds them up for the camera and reads,
60—you'll never be this young again,
from his friend. I Glove You, on a pair
of gardening gloves, from his wife.
Orange omelette with raspberries, pâté,
Caesar salad, croissants, marmalade, coffee.
Whoever said what the soul misses most is food
is right. So he didn't get the anchovies.
So he can't eat all he wants from the dessert tray.
From here on this is enough, a tableful
of food, the Hogarth prints,
the anti-rejection drugs in his wife's purse.

SHE ASKS IF I LOVE HER

There's an edge on everything,
though no one we know is dying abruptly,
and our parents, finally gone complacent
with TV and each other,
have settled down to their years.
We, too, have joined our habits
and are happy in a way.

It wasn't always so.

Down in the basement,
above that chest of a freezer,
my brother and I kept the one pair of boxing gloves
hung by their laces on a thick nail
hammered into the concrete. When we hated
each other for some childhood cruelty,
I would put on the right-hand glove

and he the left. And though we knew our father

would beat us for fighting, we would circle
and jab. Circle and jab.
I can feel my eyes swell.
I can taste the blood. I can hear
the freezer squeal like a buzzer kicking on.
The dark paneling glows. I would cradle his chin
in my free hand and kiss him, and he would hold me.

I have come to mistrust any subsequent version.

THE UNMET NEEDS

My wife's been away for three days.
I know she'll be back tomorrow, but honestly
I want to make love right now. I fry a medium egg
with lots of onion and eat it very greasy.
I don't want to have children anyway.

I'm scared. Three lonely nights. The egg doesn't help.
I want her body over mine, her dark hair going gray in my face.
I know my back will ache the next morning. I don't care.
I don't care. Flat my spare. Cut my hair. I don't care.
I want to tell her not to worry. My head cold's much better,

and I'm not soaking the wooden spoons in the sink
with the rest of the dirty dishes. I'm not interested in cable TV
or ball games. Outside, the leaves turn fantastical colors
in Kentucky, but the mountains tell me nothing useful
except the obvious: It's a poor life for poor people

separated from their loved ones. How many of us
are waiting? Someone must have the number written on a slip of paper
in a jacket pocket. The water in the vase stinks, but the wild flowers
I picked for her are still pretty. Someone must know their names.
I melt like a lozenge under my own tongue.

PUBLIC WORKS

Blue smoke settles along the hillsides
Like last year's leaves. Floyd County
Is clearing Beaver Creek to make way
For the spring rains. The workers
In brown coveralls have their orders:
Clear everything from saplings to beaver dams
To bias-ply tires. Everything must be cut down
Or burned or hauled off to control the flash floods.
So farewell to the abandoned cabin with its tin roof
Rusty and defiant that kept dry calico grannies
And their butter churns. Good riddance
To the rebel flag that marks the spot with an X
Beneath the cliff where the saw and the bulldozer
And the fire proclaim the cleanup has begun.

FOUND POEM FROM A BOOK IN A BOX OF BOOKS I SOLD TO A NOVEL IDEA BEFORE MOVING TO KENTUCKY AGAIN

for Cinnamon Dokken

Setting off from the islands in early summer, the boats sailed south along the coastline after the migrating fish, ending up in East Anglia at the end of the year. The women traveled south in special trains to work at gutting and packing the herring catch. These women worked in crews of three, continuing late into the night if the catch was large. Standing in front of a wooden trough, two of them gutted while the third packed the fish between layers of salt. Their fingers bound in bandages to protect themselves against their razor-sharp knives and the rough salt, their clothes covered in fish guts and scales, the women worked at phenomenal speed. To earn a living wage required a skilled crew to pack thirty barrels of fish a day, one fish every five seconds through the course of a ten-hour day. In the early years of the century, these women were paid eleven or twelve shillings a week, with their lodgings and travel thrown in. Despite the harshness of their working conditions, many looked back on these days with affection and nostalgia for the comradeship of their fellows.

SAFE-T-MAN

(from United Airlines High Street Emporium)

Give the appearance of having a driving companion,
or someone with whom to have your tea.
Dress him any way your mood dictates.

Today, he can be a basketball fan
with a GO WILDCATS sweatshirt.
Maybe you like the seed cap and the jacket.

Tomorrow, Safe-T-Man can be in business,
with silk tie and a blue suit,
an Armani if you can afford it,

something from Sears if you can't.
No need to consider his favorite color,
his mood, or what he wants for dinner.

You paid for him, you loaded him
into the front seat beside you
or sat him at your dining room table,

which you also earned without his help.
The city can be a dangerous place.
Safe-T-Man's available in light skin and blonde hair,

light skin and gray hair, or dark skin and dark hair.
He looks approximately 180 pounds.
The button-on legs (specify light or dark)

and the zippered carrying bag are optional.
No one knows better than you and the police
the value of a visual deterrent. Caress the air-brushed

facial highlights, rub the latex head and neck,
love this life-size dummy in proportion
to your own legitimate needs.

THE MASONRY PROFESSOR AT
THE COMMUNITY COLLEGE

The plumb bob's a difficult tool,
but so's the level, the air-bubble-
in-the-glass-tube kind I mean.
The key's to let the plumb bob
get perfectly still. Have a smoke
while you're waiting. Hey, where else
can you get paid a union wage
to stand around with your hands
in your pockets? Somebody says
something to you, just point to that
quivering air bubble in the glass tube
like it was about to predict
the stock market. Tell 'em a story,
something familiar that they think
they know, but really don't, the way
some people think they know how to lay
one brick on top of another.
You could tell 'em, for instance, that
Christ was a mason, not a carpenter.
Makes sense, doesn't it? After all
there are a hell of a lot more stones
in Galilee than trees. There's nothing
like a good story at the right moment
to get a nervous guy, who's paying
a hundred grand or so for a house,
to lighten up. Don't worry.
You'll get the hang of it. Once
you get a true, level reading,
it's impossible to make a mistake.
Just start laying down the mud with your
trowel and tell the apprentice
to keep plenty of bricks near at hand.
He's probably some college kid on break,
dreaming for a job that'll let him sit

on his ass all day. Doctor, lawyer,
professor, whatever. He's working
for you now, and at half your pay.
Remember what I told you about
keeping the mud just slick enough
to slip off the trowel nice and cleanlike.
Laying good brick and block's no secret.
The talent comes in keeping at it
long enough until the hours
and the dollars and the bricks all balance
in your flickering air bubble.
That's what most people don't understand.

TO OUR UNBORN CHILD
for Pam

Each moment 58,000 people are airborne.
Everywhere you, your mother, and I travel,
the airports and parking lots are expanding.
It's a big, worrisome world. Fields, cities,
lakes, rivers spread out below and around.
Still, you will never be too far from us.
I believe that no one asks to be born,
and yet you are scheduled to arrive.
I will not ask for your forgiveness,
nor regret my love for your sweet mother.
She hums through the turbulence, and I know
that her voice is your voice made definite.
You are content to our form.   Wife says *yes*,
and in so saying, you as well say *yes*.

TO THE DRIVER WHO TOOK MY RESERVED PARKING SPACE #53

My wife calls the office to ask if we can have lunch.
Sure, I say. Good, she says, I'll bring something. Fine.
Myself, I walk to work, but when my wife visits, my reserved
parking space #53 makes her happier than a dozen roses.

I will not sit idly by and have her made upset by the melting
ice cream bars or the cooling chicken and mashed potatoes.
I won't tolerate her frustrated walk across the August blacktop,
our lunch in hand, her mind set fixedly on her pregnant belly

while our car sits double-parked beneath a sapping maple tree.
When you return to your red Mustang, when you put the key
in the ignition, may the motor refuse to turn over and the mystery
of your clicking noises baffle even NPR's Click and Clack.

May you pick up your cell phone and may its batteries
be dead. When you step out of your car, may a sudden shower
descend upon the land. And just so my wife knows that I am
not as vengeful as her King Saul who famously demanded 100 foreskins

of his enemies, at that moment may a wrecker arrive. May my father
be the driver who steps out in the rain and looks at you, drenched
through and through, and without a word may you realize that it's all
your fault, and that from now on you will never be able to do anything
          right.

TRANSLATION OF A MATHEMATICAL EQUATION WHICH I FOUND ON A BLACKBOARD

Good morning, Mr. Tim Skeen. I don't mean
the other four Tim Skeens you find if you
search AltaVista. Not Tim Skeen the potter,
or Tim Skeen obsessed with Princess Diana,

or Tim Skeen in search of long-lost high school friends,
or Tim Skeen the equestrian—I mean you,
the Tim Skeen who quit high school algebra
after binomial equations for the pleasure

of planking in woodshop. I'm the language
you never learned, a form of metaphysical speech.
For example, when I say Good morning,
I really mean, Good morning, you schmuck.

Think of all you're missing, the exotic relationship
of positives and negatives defined with clarity
and impersonal authority. Perhaps your daughter
will pick up where you left off. Maybe she'll save

the family's reputation. One day you might walk
into a room where she's studying. You'll notice
she's laughing quietly, the knuckle of her right hand
absently in her mouth. She's reading a book,

The Joy of Fractals, something you'll never understand.
She's laughing harder now. In fact, tears are coming
to her eyes. She hears you. She looks over her shoulder
and sees you. You look into those blue eyes.

Your twenty-three chromosomes recognize themselves,
and you suddenly realize she feels sorry for you.

Tears of pity. Do you pray? Each time you walk
into this room and talk to students about language,

just remember how lucky you are to have a wife
who doesn't mind that $1 + 1$
will not always equal 2. Think of her patience
with your ignorance. How her every kind action

or word is a form of charity, of penance
for having married a numerically illiterate man
who was fortunate enough to get a scholarship
to a college where astronomy substituted for algebra.

Why don't you put down that eraser?
Why don't you leave me on the board? No?
You always were a hardhead. Go ahead, erase me.
The formulas of brilliance are as rare as moonrocks.

THE LAST CENTURY SEEN AS A USED BOOK

I set up the coffeepot
for the morning, wash the dishes,
lay out my clothes for work.

We're too tired to make love tonight.
Instead, there's the used biography
of Ehrich Weiss, Harry Houdini,
a dollar recklessly spent, perhaps,

but still only a dollar.
One arm at her side, the other,
forearm gliding over forehead,

my wife reaches to turn the page.
Submerged upside down in a can
of blurry water, Houdini slips out
of the handcuffs and says,

"When I go, I'll be gone for good.
I won't even try to come back."
Anyone could make the same mistake.

FOR THE RECORD

And these forms are so numerous, often so original, that after a positive
examination of the shell world, the imagination is defeated by reality.
— Gaston Bachelard

Vulgarity saved me,
and an innate lack of rhythm.
Putting one clubfoot in front of another

I followed you from the Chesapeake Bay
to the Great Plains of Nebraska.
I couldn't carry a tune

but you sang songs filled with wild flowers
and cultivated roses, arrowheads and seashells.
A lack of ambition, plain and simple, saved me

while you labored on a life story
which became increasingly strange
because it included the need for children.

Today, in a town you've never visited,
a female vomits blood at Mountain Manor,
an accident without injuries

is reported in the parking lot of Food City
where an employee watches a suspicious blue car
circling the parking lot,

and a man you used to love
makes the atonal confession that children
justify song, ambition, and love.

TIM SKEEN was born in the coal-mining region of eastern Kentucky. He grew up in Lorain, Ohio, where his father had migrated to find work at the local steel mill. After working as a soldier and laborer, Skeen eventually earned a Ph.D. from the University of Nebraska-Lincoln. In 1996, he returned to Appalachia to teach. For ten years, he has also served as a national disaster volunteer for the American Red Cross. He lives in Prestonsburg, Kentucky, with his wife, Pam Weiner, and daughter, Iris.